The strange

The Dunmow flitch

J. W. Robertson Scott

Alpha Editions

This edition published in 2024

ISBN : 9789362993670

Design and Setting By
Alpha Editions
www.alphaedis.com
Email - info@alphaedis.com

Contents

INTRODUCTION

Although, as in duty bound, a member of his county Archæological Society, no claim to what may be dignified by antiquarian research is made by the Author of this modest publication.

If he is entitled to any credit at all, it can be merely in respect of the fact that (in addition to making the best use of the historical stores and constant kindness of Mr. Hastings Worrin), he has regarded it as a kind of minor act of local patriotism to try to gather together and set forth, in as simple and attractive a fashion as possible, such data as, with a little trouble, may be collected concerning a Custom all the surviving records of which are of interest and importance to those who live in Great or Little Dunmow or their vicinity.

The subject has, however, a wider appeal. It is so familiar that throughout the land there can be few persons who have never heard of the Dunmow Flitch. It is so old as to be enshrined, for as long as English Literature shall endure, in Chaucer and Langland.

It is proper to mention, perhaps, that most of the subjects illustrated have not before been photographed for publication.

For corrections or for any light on difficulties still confronting the historian of the Flitch, the Author will be greatly obliged.

In order to save labour to other students of the subject, he may perhaps mention that he has searched the following MSS. at the British Museum: "Registrum Cartarum Prioratus de Dunmawe," "Exscripta è Chronico de Dunmow," "Collectanea ex Chronico de Dunmowe," "Excerpta ex Chronico de Parva Dunmowe," "Memorandum de Pernis, a Prioratu de Dunmowe," the household accounts of the last Prior of Dunmow, and "Transcripta ex Libro Rubeo in Scarrario," and has glanced through certain Court Rolls. One list of presentations of the Bacon (which appears in Leland) is described in the catalogue at the British Museum as "perhaps a fragment of some larger work on the subject." Does it still exist?

GREAT CANFIELD, DUNMOW. *Christmas*, 1909.

CHAPTER I
A NARRATIVE OF NINE HUNDRED YEARS

Everybody knows that delightful Shakespearean scene in which Sir John Falstaff robs the travellers at Gadshill. But some readers of the play must have been puzzled a little by the sorry Knight's ejaculation—

"On, bacons, on!"

From the Conquest, however, it had been common to call the multitude hogs. To this practice, it has been declared, we owe the phrase "to save one's bacon." Is not bacon the back and sides of the hog—the part, therefore, on which a blow would generally fall? And is not "to save one's bacon," obviously, to escape a blow?

But it is possible that "to save one's bacon" may have had, in part at any rate, another origin. In "The Wife of Bath's Prologue" in the *Canterbury Tales*, which were given to the world as long ago as the fourteenth century, Chaucer's free-spoken dame says—

The bacon wae not fet for hem, I trow,
That som men have in Essex at Donmow.

May not this conceivably be the Bacon of the popular saying?

The curious Dunmow Custom, by which a Flitch of Bacon has been given to married folk who have sworn that, for a year and a day, they have neither had differences nor wished themselves unwed, is certainly very old.

It may, indeed, have come over with the Conqueror. More than one book of antiquities avers that "at the abbey of Saint Melaine near Rennes"—the old capital of Brittany—there had been hanging, for more than six centuries, a side of Bacon "still quite fresh," which had been set apart for the first pair who "for a year and a day had lived without dispute and grumbling" and without repenting of their marriage.

To the Dunmow Custom we have a reference not only in old Chaucer, but in that great song of England, The Vision of William concerning Piers the Plowman, written under the shadow of the Black Death. Says the good Langland—

Many a couple since the Pestilence
Have plighted them together;
The fruit that they bring forth
Is foul words

In jealousy without happiness,
And quarrelling in bed;
They have no children but strife,
And slapping between them,
And though they go to Dunmow
(Unless the Devil help!)
To follow after the Flitch
They never after obtain it;
And unless they both are perjured,
They lose the bacon.[*]

[*] The last four lines appear as follows in the "C-text" of Professor Skeat's monumental two volume edition of the poem—

Thauh thei don hem to Donemowe . bote the deuel hem helpe
To folwen for the flicche . feccheth thei hit neuere;
Bote thei bothe be for-swore . that bacon thei tyne.

Then in *Reliquiae Antiquae*, which dates back to the fifteenth century, another poet, discoursing in relation to the Seventh Commandment, laments that he can

      fynd no man that will enquere
The parfyte wais unto Dunmow;
For they repent them within a year,
And many within a week and souner men trow.

Yet another century later one Howell says choicely—

Do not fetch your wife from Dunmow
For so you may bring home two sides of a sow!

In fact, up and down our literature there are plenty of references to the Dunmow Flitch.

CHAPTER II
THE PRIORY AND THE RHYMESTER

The gravest historians have given accounts of the beginnings of the Dunmow Custom. There is Dugdale, for instance, who was born in 1686. He writes in his *Monasticon*—

Robert Fitzwalter, who lived long beloved by King Henry, the son of King John (as also of all the realm), betook himself in his latter days to prayer and deeds of charity, and great and bountiful alms to the poor, kept great hospitality, and re-edified the decayed Priory of Dunmow, which Juga, a most devout and religious woman, had builded; in which Priory arose a custom, began and instituted either by him or some of his ancestors, which is verified by the common saying or proverb, "that he which repents him not of his marriage, either sleeping or waking, in a year and a day, may lawfully go to Dunmow and fetch a Gammon of Bacon." It is certain that such a custom there was, and that the Bacon was delivered with such solemnity and triumph as they of the Priory and Town could make— continuing till the dissolution of that house. The party or pilgrim took the Oath before the Prior of the Convent, and the Oath was administered with long process and much solemn singing and chanting.

But how did the Custom actually come about? Harrison Ainsworth has explained convincingly in his rhyme, *The Custom of Dunmow*—

"What seek you here, my children dear?
   Why kneel ye down thus lowly
Upon the stones, beneath the porch
   Of this our Convent holy?"
The Prior old the pair bespoke
   In faltering speech, and slowly.

Their modest garb would seem proclaim
   The pair of low degree,
But though in cloth of frieze arrayed,
   A stately youth was he;
While she, who knelt down by his side,
   Was beautiful to see.

"A Twelvemonth and a Day have fled
   Since first we were united;
And from that hour," the young man said,
   "No change our hopes has blighted.

Fond faith with fonder faith we've paid.
  And love with love requited.

"True to each other have we been;
  No dearer object seeing,
Than each has in the other found;
  In everything agreeing.
And every look, and word, and deed
  That breed dissension fleeing.

"All this we swear, and take in proof
  Our Lady of Dunmow!*
For She, who sits with saints above,
  Well knows that it is so.
Attest our Vow, thou reverend man,
  And bless us ere we go!"

* The accent in Dunmow is on the first syllable, not as placed by Ainsworth
and other rhymers.

The Prior old stretch'd forth his hands;
  "Heaven prosper ye!" quoth he;
"O'er such as ye, right gladly we
  Say '*Benedicite!*'"
On this, the kneeling pair uprose—
  Uprose full joyfully.

Just then, pass'd by the Convent cook—
  And moved the young man's glee;
On his broad back a mighty Flitch
  Of Bacon brown bore he.
So heavy was the load, I wis,
  It scarce mote carried be.

"Take ye that Flitch," the Prior cried,
  "Take it, fond pair, and go;
Fidelity, like yours, deserves
  The boon I now bestow.
Go, feast your friends, and think upon
  The Convent of Dunmow."

"Good Prior," then the youth replied,
  "Thy gift to us is dear,
Not for its worth, but that it shows
  Thou deem'st our love sincere,
And in return broad lands I give—
  Broad lands thy Convent near;

Which shall to thee and thine produce
  A Thousand Marks a year!

"But this Condition I annex,
  Or else the Grant's forsaken;
That whensoe'er a pair shall come,
  And take the Oath we've taken,
They shall from thee and thine receive
  A goodly Flitch of Bacon.

"And thus from out a simple chance
  A usage good shall grow;
And our example of true love
  Be held up evermo:
While all who win the prize shall bless
  The Custom of Dunmow."

STOTHARD'S PICTURE, "THE PROCESSION OF THE FLITCH OF BACON."—It was published in 1833 and was dedicated to Samuel Rogers, the poet.

STOTHARD'S PICTURE, "THE PROCESSION OF THE FLITCH OF BACON."

STOTHARD'S PICTURE, "THE PROCESSION OF THE FLITCH OF BACON."—It was published in 1833 and was dedicated to Samuel Rogers, the poet.

STOTHARD'S PICTURE ADAPTED, WITH QUEEN VICTORIA
AND PRINCE ALBERT AS LEADING ACTORS.—Among
the figures are Lord Brougham, Lord Palmerston, the Duke of
Wellington, Sir Robert Peel, Lord John Russell, the Archbishop of Canterbury and the Dukes of Sussex and Cambridge. Date of print, 1841.

STOTHARD'S PICTURE ADAPTED, WITH QUEEN VICTORIA
AND PRINCE ALBERT AS LEADING ACTORS.

STOTHARD'S PICTURE ADAPTED, WITH QUEEN
VICTORIA AND PRINCE ALBERT AS LEADING ACTORS.—
Among the figures are Lord Brougham, Lord Palmerston, the Duke
of Wellington, Sir Robert Peel, Lord John Russell, the Archbishop
of Canterbury and the Dukes of Sussex and Cambridge. Date of
print, 1841.

"Who art thou, son?" the Prior cried,
    His tones with wonder falter—
"Thou should'st not jest with reverend men,
    Nor with their feelings palter."
"I jest not, Prior, for know in me
    Sir Reginald Fitzwalter.

"I now throw off my humble garb,
    As I what I am, contest;
The wealthiest I of wealthy men,
    Since with this treasure blest."
And as he spoke, Fitzwalter clasp'd
    His lady to his breast.

"In peasant guise my love I won,
    Nor knew she whom she wedded;
In peasant cot our truth we tried,
    And no disunion dreaded.
Twelve months' assurance proves our faith
    On firmest base is steadied."

Joy reigned within those Convent walls
    When the glad news was known;
Joy reigned within Fitzwalter's halls
    When there his bride was shown.
No lady in the land such sweet
    Simplicity could own;
A natural grace had she, that all
    Art's graces far outshone:
Beauty and worth for want of birth
    Abundantly atone.

L'ENVOY

What need of more? That Loving Pair
    Lived long and truly so;
Nor ever disunited were;—
    For one death laid them low!
And hence arose that Custom old—
    The Custom of Dunmow.

Of this Fitzwalter we shall hear later on.

CHAPTER III
A YEOMAN, A HUSBANDMAN AND THOMAS LE FULLER

Now all may have fallen out exactly as Harrison Ainsworth tells us; but then, again, as Uncle Remus says, "it moughtn't."

"Among the jocular tenures of England," writes Grose—he was the antiquary for whom Burns wrote "Tam o' Shanter"—"none has been more talked about than the Bacon of Dunmow." (A peppercorn rent, which still appears in legal documents, is a kind of "jocular tenure.") In the theory of a jocular tenure we have probably the true origin of the Flitch custom.

Morant, the historian of Essex, seems to think that this was the case. He writes—

The Prior and Canons were obliged to deliver the Bacon to them that took the Oath, by virtue (as many believe) of a Founder or Benefactor's Deed or Will, by which they held lands, rather than of their own singular frolic and wantonness, or more probably it was imposed by the Crown, either in Saxon or Norman times, and was a burthen upon their estate.

It is explained that "after the Pilgrims, as the Claimants were called, had taken the Oath, they were taken through the Town in a Chair, on Men's Shoulders, with all the Friars, Brethren, and Townsfolk, young and old, male and female after them, with shouts and acclamations, and the Bacon was borne before them on poles."

The Chartulary of Dunmow Priory (*Registrum Cartarum Prioratus de Dunmawe*), a thickish quarto, clearly written in old contracted Latin, is still to be seen any day in the British Museum. There are two entries in reference to the Flitch. One is dated 1445, the other 1510. The first is on page 128 and the other on the opening page. Both are among collections of memoranda apart from the actual Chartulary, which itself contains no reference to the Flitch. (*See* Appendix.) Here are translations of the entries—

Memorandum: that one Richard Wright, of Badbourge, near the City of Norwich, in the County of Norfolk, Yeoman, came and required the Bacon of Dunmow on the 17th day of April, in the 23rd year of the reign of King Henry VI, and according to the form of the charter, was sworn before John Cannon, Prior of this place and the Convent, and many other neighbours, and there was delivered to him, the said Richard, one Flitch of Bacon.

Memorandum: that in the year of our Lord, 1510, Thomas le Fuller, of Coggeshall, in the County of Essex, came to the Priory of Dunmow, and on the 8th September, being Sunday, in the second year of King Henry VIII, he was, according to the form of the Charter, sworn before John Tylor, the Prior of the house and Convent, as also before a multitude of neighbours, and there was delivered unto him, the said Thomas, a Gammon of Bacon.

On a sheet pasted on the last page of a volume of MSS. consisting of extracts from the Red Book of the Exchequer ("Transcripta ex Libro Rubeo in Scarrario"), the foregoing entries are recorded in cramped English, and also a third, which, as a matter of fact, is written first—

Memorandum: that one Stephen Samuel, of Little Easton, in the County of Essex, Husbandman, came to the Priory of Dunmow, on our Lady-day in Lent, in the Seventh year of King Edward IV, and required a Gammon of Bacon, and was sworn before Roger Bulcott, then Prior, and the Convent of this place, as also before a multitude of other neighbours, and there was delivered to him a Gammon of Bacon.

It will be seen that in two cases it was a Gammon not a Flitch of Bacon that was awarded. (A Flitch is a side, a Gammon a leg of Bacon.)

It is also of interest to notice that, in the cases reported, the Bacon is given to a man, not to a husband and wife. An historian also speaks of "the Pilgrim" and of "*his* Bacon being borne before *him*."

The first recorded presentation of the Bacon is dated, as will be observed, 1445. But, in view of the allusion in Chaucer a century before, it is plain that the custom must have existed even before his time. The references to the custom in other early authors would also seem to point to the fact of it having been frequently observed. There are, however, only three gifts of the Bacon noted down in the documents of the Priory, now in the care of the British Museum.

CHAPTER IV
THE VANISHED CLOISTERS

There is little now to be seen of the old Priory spoken of by Leland.

Approached from the hamlet, the existing Priory Church of Little Dunmow, with its roof of staring blue slates, its factory chimney-like bell tower and mean walling, attracts attention only by its oddity. But when one walks up the farm land from which the south side of the building may be viewed, one receives a different impression. In the architecture now seen there are the

lines where beauty lingers,

the lines which tell of a splendid structure. The remains of no common building stand in solitary domination of these quiet corn fields.

One enters the church and is surprised, as Mr. Hartley has written, by that

indefinable feeling which ever strikes us on our entry into a spacious and beautiful edifice. That the building is a fragment of what must have been a structure of extreme beauty becomes evident. Columns of such dimensions and arches of such design were never intended for purpose so slight as the support of the present roof; windows of such size and elegance were made for shedding light upon a much more spacious interior than we now find.

But when account is taken of all the stately arches and columns, and the beautifully cut ornament thereon, now embodied in the brick rubble and plaster which we owe to Georgian and Early Victorian dulness and parsimony, no more of the old Priory survives for our refreshment than the south aisle of the choir. The stones of the structure that were hewn and raised by some "Master Henry" or "Master Hubert the Mason," the timbers that some "Master John the Carpenter" industriously wrought, even the marble and alabaster which crowned the work have long been torn away. They are come upon now, in fragments in the walls and floors and roofs of cottages and barns which adjoin the church.

SCENE AT THE MODERN CEREMONY.—The Trial proceeding. Judge in the middle. Two pairs of claimants on either side. Counsel for the claimants speaking; counsel for the Bacon seated. Jury of maidens and bachelors on extreme right. Highly entertained public in front at 1s. a head.

SCENE AT THE MODERN CEREMONY.

SCENE AT THE MODERN CEREMONY.—The Trial Proceeding. Judge in the Middle. Tow pairs of claimants on either side. Counsel for the claimants speaking; counsel for the Bacon seated. Jury of maidens and bachelors on extreme right. Highly entertained public in front at 1s. a head.

PROCESSION AFTER THE MODERN CEREMONY.—Two couples in chairs, recent imitations of the original in the Priory Church. The Bacon is swinging from poles behind the second couple.

PROCESSION AFTER THE MODERN CEREMONY.

PROCESSION AFTER THE MODERN CEREMONY.—Two couples in chairs, recent imitations of the original in the Priory Church. The Bacon is swinging from poles behind the second couple.

Where the monastic building once extended nothing remains but the out of sight foundations which try the patience of the digger of land drains. Labourers' patches of potatoes and greens range over consecrated ground. The fishponds of the monks, to which they had recourse "on Fridays when they fasted," grow grass or bear the burden of a railway embankment. Tradition and propinquity, but these only, point to venerable cottages and a farmhouse as marking the position of the Priory's Manor house and Grange.

Of memorials of the Flitch ceremony two are shown—the oaken seat, in which successful applicants for the Bacon were chaired, and the stones on which they knelt.

The chair is kept within the altar rails. Two persons could no doubt be squeezed into it. There are holes in the chair through which the bearers' poles went.

Whether the chair belonged originally to the Prior and was actually used when he gave away the Flitch, or was the property of one of the Lords of the Manor, who, after the Dissolution of the Monasteries, continued the custom, has been disputed. But there is evidence pointing to the chair having been employed on the occasion of the Manorial awards only. Mr. F. Roe, in his *Old Oak Furniture*, though he attributes the chair to the thirteenth century, doubts very much whether it can have been used from the beginning for the ritual of the Flitch. For this reason—

The outer right-hand side of the chair is carved with wheel-like decorations, but on the left-hand side the surface of the wood is plain, and various mortices are visible, which show that the seat is part of a larger structure, being, in fact, the end unit of a series of stalls. The truth is that the chair used by merry-makers at the ceremony of the Flitch, is actually a waif from the conventual establishment. It is, one is bound to admit, a remarkable coincidence that the chair and ceremony should have had their origin in the same reign, but the fact that it is only part of some fitted furniture, precludes the possibility of it having been designed for the purpose for which it was used in later years.

In the accounts available of the awarding of the Flitch after the closing of the religious houses by Henry VIII we hear of "two great stones near the Church door" on which the applicant for the Bacon had to kneel. Whether they are still in existence is uncertain.

What are to-day pointed out as the stones on which the Pilgrims knelt may possibly be the bases of two of the many columns which local vandals in want of building material have demolished. They are certainly not "sharp," as some chroniclers describe the stones to have been. A pair of stones like those in the Church are to be seen in Little Dunmow village.

In Hone's *Table Book*, published about the time of the accession of Queen Victoria, it is said that "the two great stones" were then in the Church. But whether the writer of this statement had actually seen them for himself does not appear. It may perhaps be mentioned that, as the first presentations of the Bacon were made seemingly not to wedded pairs but to husbands only, there could not be at this early stage of the history of the Custom any need for "two" stones. The present stones are each only about half a foot in diameter and the right distance apart for one person to kneel on them. They could hardly be described as "great" stones.

CHAPTER V
A TALE OF TYRANNY AND WAR

Below the pavement of the Priory Church many dead sleep. Four graves only are marked by stones. One resting-place, supposed to be that of the Lady Juga, the foundress of the Priory, is covered by a slab of grey marble "coffin-fashioned, with a cross flory." Over three other tombs are mutilated alabaster effigies, once "heedlessly thrown among heaps of bricks and rubbish."

Begun, Dugdale and Morant say, in 1104, the Priory was more than a century a-building. Indeed, it was as late as 1501 that "five bells were blessed in Dunmow steeple." Only thirty-four years were to pass before the Dissolution of the Monasteries. It is doubtful if the Priory was even then finished. In fact, in the expenses of the Priory for 1534 are payments to two men "for making of ix foote of the stepull." (*See* Appendix.)

We have seen how much now remains of the scene whereon the Prior and his dozen Augustinian monks prayed and ruled on revenues drawn from holdings of land in four counties.

The Lady Juga was sister to one Ralph Baynard who came over from Normandy with William. Among the twenty-five Essex lordships which his sovereign gave him were those of Great and Little Dunmow. When the grandson of this Baynard fell out with Henry I, it was not long before that energetic monarch had a Fitzwalter enjoying the advantages of the lordships.

Fitzwalters followed one another for ten generations. The family is notable for the "Sir Reginald Fitzwalter" of Harrison Ainsworth's ballad. Tradition has long declared him to be old Dugdale's Lord Robert who "re-edified the decayed Priory of Dunmow." He had the generalship of that "Army of God and Holy Church" which wrung Magna Charta from John in 1215, and was "the first champion of English liberty."

This knight (says Newcourt) lived in all affluence of Riches and Honour, 16y and ob. 1234, 19 Hen. III, and was buried before the High Altar in this Priory Church near his said daughter, the Fair Matilda.

The battered and chopped effigy of the Fitzwalter now lying by the side of his wife in the church is no longer said to be, however, but rather the bearer of the name who died in 1432.

The remaining figure in the church may or may not represent the "Fair Matilda." A stern archæologist has suggested, indeed, that it is the effigy of the wife of the second of the Fitzwalters. But the touching and beautiful expression of the alabaster face goes well with what history and tradition tell us of the lovely Matilda, and with the tale originally told in the *Dunmow Chronicle.*

Legend has made her the "Maid Marian" whom Friar Tuck united to Robin Hood, and the story is set forth in a novel by the author of the once-esteemed *Proverbial Philosophy.*

"Maid Marian" is, however, as Dr. Brewer points out, the boy in the Morris dance, and is so called from the morion which he wore on his head. ("A set of morrice dancers," says Temple, "danced a maid marian.")

But the story of the pursuit of the beautiful daughter of Fitzwalter by John has been thought to be well founded. Upon her father resisting the King he was dispossessed of all his property. Other barons took sides against the sovereign, and Newcourt writes that Fitzwalter fled into France. John, having spoiled the castles of those who resisted him,

sent a messenger to the fair Matilda now remaining here in Dunmow about hie old suit in love, and because she would not agree to his wicked motion, the messenger poison'd a boil'd or poch'd egg against she was hungry and gave it to her, whereof she died, and was buried here in the choir at Dunmow, between two pillars in the S. side thereof.

Another story is that the King sent Matilda a pair of poisoned gloves. (*See* Appendix.)

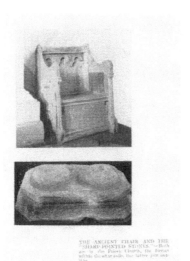

THE ANCIENT CHAIR AND THE
"SHARP-POINTED STONES."—Both
are in the Priory Church, the former
within the altar rails, the latter just outside.

THE ANCIENT CHAIR AND THE "SHARP-POINTED STONES."

THE ANCIENT CHAIR AND THE "SHARP-POINTED STONES."—Both are in the Priory Church, the former within the altar rails, the latter just outside.

THE EFFIGIES IN THE PRIORY CHURCH.—
Traditionally regarded as representing the founder of
the Priory church and his wife, and the "Fair Matilda"
poisoned by King John. There is no doubt that the knight
is one of the Beauchamps, and that the female figure done
by itself represents a member of the same house. An
interment in 1347 recorded in the registers of the Church
is described as "next to the tomb of Matilda."

THE EFFIGIES IN THE PRIORY CHURCH.

THE EFFIGIES IN THE PRIORY CHURCH.—Traditionally regarded as representing the founder of the Flitch custom and his wife, and the "Fair Matilda" poisoned by King John. There is no doubt that the knight is one of the Fitzwalters, and that the female figure lying by itself represents a member of the same house. An interment in 1627 recorded in the Register of the Church is described as "next to the tomb of Matilda."

Then the King of France (Newcourt goes on) also began to waste his (King John's) dominions, but a day of reconciliation being appointed between the two Kings, King John passed over into France, and the two Armies were parted by an arm of the sea.

Then an English knight went out and challenged any to break a spear for his mistress's sake. Robert Fitzwalter came over, and, encountering with his great Lance, overthrew both the Knight and the Horse, and so returned to the King of France.

Then said King John, by God's Troth, he were a King indeed who had such a Knight in his Retinue. His friends, hearing this, knelt before the King and said, Sir, he is your Own Knight, and ready at your command, Robert Fitzwalter. The next day he restored to him his Barony with all appurtenances, and the two Kings were reconciled by the interposition of Robert, and all the banished persons were recalled, with leave to rebuild their castles.

"The death of Robin Hood with the lamentable Tragedie of Chaste Matilda, his faire Maid Marian poisoned at Dunmowe by King John," printed in 1601, is one of two plays on the subject, and is reprinted by Hazlitt. Michael Drayton wrote poetical accounts of the story, and in 1639 Robert Davenport produced a third play, "King John and Matilda."

CHAPTER VI

THE JURY OF SPINSTERS

The last Prior of Dunmow was Geoffry Shether.* After the Dissolution of the Monasteries, the duty of giving the Bacon seems to have passed to the Lords of the Manor of Little Dunmow. They held their Courts—as they have been held within living memory—at Priory Place, formerly a farmhouse and now four cottages. In a parchment book belonging to a former Lord of the Manor, the Rev. James Hughes-Hallett, and now in the possession of Mr. de Vins Wade of Great Dunmow, the present Lord of the Manor, there is an account of the Bacon ceremonies which was written in 1737.

* See Appendix.

It is therein stated that the custom was first instituted by the monks "in ye year 1111 and continued to this day." The "two hard stones" are described as "yet to be seen in the doorway of the Pryory," and it is explained that "the oath was administered with such long process, and such solemn singing over him, as doubtless must make his Pilgrimage Painfull."

If it be true that the ceremony took place, as described, "before the whole Towns," and that the successful applicant for the Bacon was "carried after through the Towns with all the Fryers and Brethren and all the Townsfolk, young and old, following them with shouts and acclamations," it would appear that Great as well as Little Dunmow had its share in the Flitch custom. The Manor of Little Dunmow extends some distance into Great Dunmow.

In the Hughes-Hallett parchment (as also in Lansdowne Roll, 25, British Museum), the Manorial ceremony is chronicled—

A Court Baron of the worshipfull Sir Thomas May, Knight, there helden of Fryday, the 27th day of June in the Thirteenth year of King William ye Third and in ye year 1701 before Thomas Wheeler, Gent., steward of the said Court.

Be it remembered that William Parsley of Much Eyston in the County of Essex and Jane his wife, being married for the space of 3 years last, past and upwards, by means of their Quiet, Peaceful, Tender and Loving

Cohabitation for the said space of time, came and claimed the Bacon, and there was delivered unto them a Gammon of Bacon.

The homage of the last mentioned were Elizabeth Beaumont, Henrietta, Annabella, Jane Beaumont and Mary Wheeler, Spinsters.

Be it remembered that att the Said Court it is found and presented by the Homage aforesaid that John Reynolds of Hatfield Regis, alias Hatfield Broadoak, in the County of Essex, gent., and Ann his wife have been married for the space of ten years last, part and upwards, and it is likewise found, presented by the Homage aforesaid that the said John Reynolds and Ann his wife by means of their Quiet, Peaceable, etc., etc.

Whereupon the said Steward, with the Jury, suitors and other officers of the Court, proceeded with the usual solemnity to the ancient and accustomed place for the Administration of the Oath (and receiving the Bacon aforesaid), that is to say to the two great stones lying near the church door within the said Manor

Whereupon the said John Reynolds and Ann kneeling down on the said two stones the said Steward did administer unto them the Oaths in these words or this effect following—

You shall swear by Custom of Confession
That you ne'er made Nuptial Transgression;
Nor since you were married Man and Wife,
By Household Brawls or Contentious Strife,
Or otherwise in Bed or att board,
Offended each other in deed or word;
Or in a Twelve month time and a Day,
Repented not in Thought any way;
Or since the Church clerk said Amen,
Wish'd yourselves unmarried again,
But continued true, and in desire,
As when you join'd hand in holy Choire.

And immediately thereupon ye said John Reynolds and Ann, claiming the said Bacon, the Court pronounced sentence for the same in these words or to the effect following, viz.—

Since to these Conditions without any fear,
Of your own accords you do truly swear;
A whole Gammon of Bacon you do receive,
And bear it away with love and good leave;
For this is the Custom at Dunmow well known.
Tho' the Pleasure be ours, the Bacon's your own.

And accordingly a Gammon of Bacon with the usual solemnity was delivered unto John Reynolds and Ann his wife.

The interesting entry follows—

"N.B.—All the above mentioned Homage and Mrs. Ann Reynolds are still living."

CHAPTER VII

—AND BACHELORS

The Dunmow Bacon ceremony is discussed in the *Spectator* of October 15, 1714, and in the succeeding number, the writer concluding—

I hope your readers are satisfied of this truth, that as love generally produces matrimony, so it often happens that matrimony produces love.

Thirty-seven years later there is a record of the giving of the Bacon by the Lord of the Manor, the recipients being Thomas Shakeshaft, of the parish of Weathersfield, Essex, weaver, and Ann his wife. They figure in the *Everyday Book* illustration. The "Hommage" on this occasion consisted of Bachelors as well as Spinsters—

HOMMAGE.

William Townsend, Gent.
Mary Cater, Spinster.
John Strutt, the younger, Gent.
Martha Wickford, Spinster
James Raymond, the younger, Gent.
Elizabeth Smith, Spinster.
Daniel Heckford, Gent.
Catherine Brett, Spinster.
Robert Mapletoft, Gent.
Eliza Hazlefoot, Spinster.
Richard Birch, Gent.
Sarah Mapletoft, Spinster.

At this ceremony—it is reported in the *Gentleman's Magazine* and the *London Magazine* of the year—some five thousand persons were present. The weaver Shakeshaft and his wife are said to have made a good deal of money by selling slices of their gammon.

Photographs of prints of scenes at the Shakeshaft presentation—one from a painting by David Ogbourne, a local artist*—are now reproduced.

* *See Essex Review*, vol. viii.

It is as well the pictorial records were made, for this ceremony of 1751 is regarded as "the last legitimate instance" of the presentation of the Bacon.

An old copperplate from Ogbourne's painting has recently been acquired by Mr. Hastings Worrin.

By the kindness of Mr. de Vins Wade we are able to furnish photographs of the receipts given by the Reynoldses and the Shakeshafts for their Bacon.

The names of the witnesses who "doe certify the proceedings" at the Shakeshaft ceremony are—Susannah Smith, Susannah Calvert, Thomas Pocklington, James Turner (? Turvin), W. Wicksted, and Mark Gretton, Curate, who is no doubt the clerical figure shown in the Ogbourne picture.

Mr. Wade's father and grandfather were stewards of the Manor, of which he is now the Lord, from 1796 to 1837, and from 1837 to 1871 respectively. Mr. de Vins Wade became steward in 1891 and Lord of the Manor by purchase in 1903. The records in Mr. Wade's possession go back to 1640.

REMAINS OF THE OLDEST PART OF THE PRIORY CHURCH.—Similar work is found in Glastonbury Abbey.

REMAINS OF THE OLDEST PART OF THE PRIORY CHURCH.

REMAINS OF THE OLDEST PART OF THE PRIORY CHURCH.—Similar work is found in Glastonbury Abbey.

INTERIOR OF PRIORY CHURCH BEFORE "RE-
STORATION."—A lithograph from a drawing by A. Barfield, of Great Dunmow, published in 1837. The square
pews, in which some of the people sat with their backs to
the parson, remained till 1872-3.

INTERIOR OF PRIORY CHURCH BEFORE "RESTORATION."

INTERIOR OF PRIORY CHURCH BEFORE
"RESTORATION."—A lithograph from a drawing by A. Barfield
of Great Dunmow, published in 1837. The square pews, in which
some of the people sat with their backs to the parson, remained till
1872-3.

CHAPTER VIII

THE BACON REFUSED

The register of the Priory Church of Little Dunmow starts with the year 1555, but it says nothing about the presentations of Bacon.

Following the Shakeshaft presentation of 1751 there is said (in Chambers's *Book of Days*) to have been an award in 1763. But Mr. Wade, on examining the records of the Manor, finds that no court was held in that year, "so," as he says, "there could not have been a proper presentation." The story seems to be incorrect. It may be mentioned that the first Essex newspaper was not started till 1764. In 1772 a couple who applied for the Flitch after due notice, and appeared with "a great concourse of people," found, "to the great disappointment of the happy couple and their numerous attendants, the Priory gates fast nailed in pursuance of the express orders of the Lord of the Manor."

Six years later, however, the Custom was sufficiently alive for there to be produced at the Haymarket Theatre a "ballad opera" called *The Flitch of Bacon*. It was the work of one Henry Bates, the son of an Essex clergyman, but was poor stuff. A better verse than most ran—

Since a year and a day
Have in love roll'd away,
   And an oath of that love has been taken,
On the sharp pointed stones.
With your bare marrow bones,
   You have won our fam'd Priory bacon.

The "poetry" written in connexion with the Flitch ceremony is indeed more remarkable for quantity than quality. Four lines, produced in 1803 and supposed to be a farmer's reply to an inquiry as to how he came by the Flitch, run—

I'll inform you, my friend, how it come.
You yourself will acknowledge the reason is clear,
As soon as I tell you that my pretty dear
Has been all her life—deaf and dumb!

It is often said that when Queen Victoria had been married a year and a day—ergo in 1841—the then Lord of the Manor privately offered a Flitch to Her Majesty, but that the compliment was declined. Mr. Wade, however, does not remember to have heard anything of the matter, and the story may have had its origin in the publication of the burlesque of Stothard's picture. In the year 1851, just a century after the Shakeshafts had had their Gammon, the Bacon was refused by the Lord of the Manor to a humbler personage, a yeoman farmer of the name of Hurrell and his wife, living at Felsted, a village lying in sight of Little Dunmow.

Thereupon, in order that the local custom should not be extinguished, it was arranged to give Mr. and Mrs. Hurrell their Bacon at a "rural fête" at Easton Park. The thing was done with an imitation of the old ceremony and with much enthusiasm, band-playing and eating and drinking, in the presence of three thousand people, "rich and poor, gentle and simple."

CHAPTER IX

ENTER THE NOVELIST

The novel, *The Flitch of Bacon: or, the Custom of Dunmow, A Tale of English Home*, was published by Harrison Ainsworth in 1854. It was dedicated to Tauchnitz of the famous Leipzig editions.

Much of the action takes place in a mythical Dunmow Flitch Inn, which is described as having once been the home of "Sir Walter Fitzwalter." The story turns largely on the desire of the four-times married landlord of this hostelry to gain the Bacon.

The house Ainsworth is thought to have had in mind is Rose Farm, a building overlooking the Church. "Monkbury Place," the Lord of the Manor's house, is imaginary, and Sir Gilbert de Montfichet—Mountfichet is a local name, however—has no place in history.

The novel is hard reading, but its publication had the effect of attracting a good deal of notice to that "Custom of Dunmow" described as "of late years discontinued." The inhabitants of Great Dunmow—in the face of "injudicious but fruitless opposition"—at length proceeded to form a Committee, and Mr. Ainsworth subscribed five guineas and the cost of two Flitches of Bacon to a fund for a revival of the ceremony.

When the notices were issued quite a number of applications were received. A Kentish veterinary surgeon and his wife were among the selected couples, but the wife died before the ceremony took place. Eventually the opportunity of presenting themselves at the "trial" was given to the Chevalier and Madame de Chatelain of London, known as translators from the French and German, and to Mr. James Barlow, a Chipping Ongar builder, and his wife.

The "jury of maidens and bachelors" sat in the Town Hall, which was decorated with flowers, and for the first time there were "Counsel for the claimants" and "for the Bacon," also a Crier who, "with mock ceremony," opened the Court.

The successful candidates were "carried in procession to a fête near the town," where Mr. Ainsworth awarded the Flitches. The management appears to have been placed in the hands of the lessee of Drury Lane.

Two years afterwards Mr. Harrison Ainsworth again presented Flitches. The candidates were Dr. and Mrs. J. N. Hawkins of Victoria Place, Regent's Park, and Jeremiah Heard, a Staffordshire policeman, and his wife.

For some reason or other the Bacon was awarded to Mr. and Mrs. Heard only; "a silver testimonial" was given to Mr. and Mrs. Hawkins. In the course of the day, we are told, Mr. Ainsworth animadverted on the action of the Lord of the Manor in "neglecting to keep up his charter."

CHAPTER X

THE WINNERS OF THE BACON

Through the instrumentality of a local Committee, awards of the Bacon were also made in 1869, 1874 and 1876. The next presentation took place in 1890. The following is a list of recipients from that year onwards—

1890. Mr. and Mrs. J. HOY, Tottenham.

1891. Rev. and Mrs. W. C. WALLACE, Shebbear Vicarage, Highampton, N. Devon.

Mr. and Mrs. WILLIAM BOWEN, Hounslow.

1892. Mr. and Mrs. JOSEPH HIRD, Turner's Road, Burdett Road, Bow.

Mr. and Mrs. D. BRIDGMAN, Tycoe Villa, Allenby Road, Forest Hill.

1893. Mr. and Mrs. F. WEBB, Needwood Villas, Falling Heath, Wednesbury.

Mr. and Mrs. PHIL. GARNER, West Molesey, Surrey.

1894. Mr. and Mrs. ANGELO FAHIE, Monketown, Dublin.

Mr. and Mrs. D. WELCH, Essenden, Herts.

1895. Sergt.-Major and Mrs. D. BAKER, Plumstead.

Mr. and Mrs. G. JOHNSON, Market Harborough.

Mr. and Mrs. CLOUGH, Surlingham, Norfolk.

1896. Mr. and Mrs. ALFRED DRURY, Queen's College, Oxford.

Mr. and Mrs. H. JOHNSON, 35, Clayton Buildings, Kennington Road, Lambeth.

Mr. and Mrs. EDWARD ROOKE, White Cottage, Hailey Lane, Great Amwell, Herts.

1897. Mr. and Mrs. J. LAMBERT, 43, Mildmay Road, Islington.

Mr. and Mrs. G. TAYLOR, Little Leighs.

1898. Mr. and Mrs. F. HERBERT, Hounslow.

Mr. and Mrs. JAMES FROST, Sutton, Surrey.

1899. Mr. and Mrs. A. McCULLOCK, Norwich.

1900. Mr. and Mrs. EVELYN J. EVATT, Newcastle.

Mr. and Mrs. J. MUNNINGS, Pinner, Middlesex.

1901. Mr. and Mrs. J. O. DEVEREUX, 62, Nelson Square, Southwark, S.E.

Mr. and Mrs. H. E. CLARKE, Stepney, E.

1902. Mr. and Mrs. G. H. WALLIS, Derby.

Mr. and Mrs. ALFRED BROOK, Bromley, Kent.

EARLY PRINTS OF THE PRIORY CHURCH.

EARLY PRINTS OF THE PRIORY CHURCH.—Top drawing by
T. M. Baynes; published 1822. Lower drawing by J. Craig.

FURTHER PRINTS OF THE PRIORY CHURCH.
—The top illustration is from an old print, undated.
The lower engraving is by J. Newton; published 1786.

FURTHER PRINTS OF THE PRIORY CHURCH.

FURTHER PRINTS OF THE PRIORY CHURCH.—The top illustration is from an old print, undated. The lower engraving is by J. Newton; published 1786.

1903. Mr. and Mrs. J. C. KEEBLE, Northampton.

Mr. and Mrs. W. L. JACKAMAN, Felixstowe.

1904. Mr. and Mrs. C. HOLFORD, Putney.

Mr. and Mrs. QUIGGIN.

1905. Rev. and Mrs. O. F. S. P. JENKINS, St. John's, Mold. N. Wales.

Mr. and Mrs. F. J. G. NOAKES, 17, Bedlum, Bitterly, Ludlow, Salop.

1906. Mr. and Mrs. W. S. J. LLOYD-WILLEY, 5, Cottage Grove, Bow, E.

Mr. and Mrs. H. LEWIS MORGAN, 517, Cliff Road, Bristol.

No ceremony has been held since 1906.

CHAPTER XI

THE SCENE AT THE MODERN CEREMONY

Humorous account of a recent Flitch festival, which appeared in the London *Star*, may be reproduced in part, as an outsider's impression of the modern ceremony—

The sun poured down on Dunmow meadows. Most of the population of the country round was gathered in holiday dress, and a steam barrel organ, which neighed a series of melodies without intermission, drove all the birds to the adjoining counties and made things sonorously cheerful. The rustics threw balls at cocoanuts, drank beer, ate cakes, and disported themselves innocently through the early hours awaiting the matrimonial inquisition.

The huge marquee tent, where the secrets of several households were to be ruthlessly laid bare, was visited by a number of chubby gentlemen who whispered mysteriously. Finally, at three o'clock all was ready, and public shillings flowed in a steady stream into the committee's hat. Soon the tent was crowded to suffocation.

There was a platform with a big chair for the judge, a bench for the claimants and tables for the counsel. There were twelve seats for the jury on the left. An assortment of functionaries walked to and fro on the stage and disappeared into side rooms through *portières* artistically constructed of old corn bags blended in tasteful harmony. Finally the *portières* swung back and the historical company appeared.

There was a Judge in scarlet and ermine wearing a full-bottomed wig which appeared to have been thoughtfully improvised overnight from a woolly grey doormat. There were two Counsel in wigs and gowns, one for the claimants and one against them. There was an Usher in a gown and fishing pole, which, it was explained to anxious enquirers, was his rod of office. This picturesque party sat down with great gravity, and looked at each other with great gravity until the jury came in.

The Jury created a sensation. It consisted of six pairs of strawberry and cream cheeks, six dimpled noses and six new straw hats. It wore other things also, including white dresses and knots of pink ribbon to indicate its official importance. It also giggled and then looked serious, but it did not all giggle at once or look serious at once.

After the young misses came six lads with knots of ribbon and feet which the owners seemed to want to get out of the way. One juryman in his despair had the courage to begin a conversation with the young jurywoman in front of him.

It is one of the rules of the Flitch that the married couples shall be judged by a Jury whose matrimonial knowledge is purely theoretical.

The first couple were a parson and his wife, both a little portly. They were a charming couple however, and had the documents to prove it. The second pair was a doctor and his wife and both wore eye-glasses. They were slender. The wife smiled pleasantly and the husband looked shrewd and good-natured. The lady belonging to the third couple seemed starched and stiff and her husband had rather a crisp expression. The first name of the male claimant in this case was William Willie. Smaller absurdities than this have been the subject of a domestic scene, but the life of Mr. and Mrs. William Willie was understood to be beautiful. Mrs. William Willie was a laundress, and William Willie occasionally helped her.

The history of each couple was given. They were all of middle age and had all been married within a few years. Mr. William Willie, it was said, fell in love with Mrs. William Willie at Hounslow, and, though called to foreign parts, returned to find her faithful.

The attorney for the claimants was an eloquent man. He spoke of Fitzwalter and other things and then he said that he was confident that his clients would safely pass the ordeal and told the jury so repeatedly, the jury giggling each time.

When the first couple stood up it was certainly very funny. The audience laughed loud and long. There is nothing very much funnier than a sedate and elderly couple being gravely questioned in the presence of hundreds of people concerning the details of their daily life. Mr. William Willie said his wife was the best woman in England, and she always sweetly bade him goodbye when he went and greeted him with a loving smile when he came. The searching questions were so absurd and were answered in such a straightforward way that the Counsel for the claimants lost control of himself and laughed till the tears rolled down his cheeks, the audience doing likewise.

Mrs. William Willie was equally straightforward but a little uncomfortable. She explained that her husband wiped his feet in muddy weather, did not smoke too much and never indulged in spirituous liquors.

Finally the Counsel, with a triumphant glance at the Jury, turned this pair over to the opposing Counsel.

Then came some impromptu repartee between Counsel, which was entirely successful. Then searching questions by the Counsel for the Bacon and more laughter. Mr. and Mrs. William Willie had testimonials from friends who had visited them to say that a cross word was unknown in their home. Counsel said that was all very well, but no one quarrelled before company. He wanted to know whether affairs were equally amicable in private. With great ingenuity he went over all the various ways in which husbands manage to ruffle the feathers of their spouses, but finally based his address to the Jury on the general valuelessness of testimonials and the all-round improbability of the whole story.

Then came another hot argument for the claimants, and the Judge summed up with great impartiality. After this the case went to the Jury.

It was awkward at first, but soon it got to whispering quite busily. Each jurywoman leaned back and was talked to by the juryman behind her, six pink ears being in such close proximity to six downy upper lips that nobody was in the least surprised when it was announced that the Jury wished to retire. It retired and it was gone many minutes. It was even feared that it had eloped, and the usher with the fishing pole was sent after it, and brought it back. It settled down with more giggles and the verdict was announced: For the claimants. And there was a storm of applause.

The other two cases passed off similarly and more quickly. Two such tender husbands and two such happy wives were never seen. It was a foregone conclusion in each case.

The chairing of the two couples through the crowds in the meadow with their Bacon swinging before them followed.

It is hardly necessary to add the comment of an historian of Essex on the attempt "to raise the ghost of the Custom": "The ceremony was only a theatrical parade of dry bones; the ancient spirit of the thing was not there—so impossible is it for society to go backward or to clothe with flesh the skeleton of an obsolete habit or dead custom, which modern feeling and refinement have long entombed."

Three years ago an imitation of the Dunmow celebration was attempted at Walthamstow.

In 1909 the farmers round about Dunmow, by co-operating to form a Dunmow Flitch Bacon Factory, carried forward the Bacon tradition on new lines.

This local record—by a Vegetarian! for *tempora mutantur*, and with the changed times which have overthrown the Flitch, *nos mutamur in illis*—should not close perhaps without the following extract from a rhyme in *Punch*. If a little better than some other poetical effusions on the subject of the Flitch, it certainly ignores the basic principle of the Flitch foundation, that it takes two to make a quarrel!—

If ever through the coming year,
   You feel a mood of deep distress,
The cause whereof may not appear
   (Maybe the cook, or cussedness);
If there should come the moment when
   You seem to lose your self-control,
And counting slowly up to ten
   Fails to relieve your soul;
If you should feel insanely prone
   To controversial debate
Till reason totters on her throne
   For pure desire to aggravate;
If you would madly say, you will,
   Merely because I hope you won't,
Dear, though it almost makes you ill,
   Think of the Flitch, and don't.

DUNMOW TOWN HALL, "COUNSEL FOR THE BACON", PRIORY
CHURCH IN 1802

DUNMOW TOWN HALL, where the ceremony presided over by Harrison Ainsworth took place.

"COUNSEL FOR THE BACON."—Mr. T. Gibbons in this rôle cross-examining a Claimant.

PRIORY CHURCH IN 1802.—From a drawing of this date, valuable as showing a part of the edifice now demolished.

IN LITTLE DUNMOW.—A typical old dwelling in Little Dunmow. It was such an one, Rose Farm, that Harrison Ainsworth had in mind in describing his Dunmow Flitch Inn.

"PRIORY PLACE."—An extremely old building now in use as cottages, where the Courts of the Lord of the Manor were held. Supposed to be on the site of the Priory Manor house.

IN LITTLE DUNMOW, "PRIORY PLACE"

IN LITTLE DUNMOW.—A typical old dwelling in Little Dunmow. It was such an one, Rose Farm, that Harrison Ainsworth had in mind in describing his Dunmow Flitch Inn.

"PRIORY PLACE."—An extremely old building now in use as cottages, where the Courts of the Lord of the Manor were held. Supposed to be on the site of the Priory Manor house.

CHAPTER XII

ANOTHER FLITCH CUSTOM

A bacon custom, not unlike that of Dunmow, existed at Wichnor, a little place near Lichfield. It originated in a jocular tenure by which Sir Philip de Somerville held the Manor from Edward III. In memory of that tenure a wooden Flitch of Bacon is displayed to this day above the great fireplace in Wichnor Hall. The oath was to the following effect—

Hear ye, Sir Philip de Somervile, lord of Whichenoure, maintainer and giver of this Bacon, that I, A, syth I wedded B, my wyfe, and syth I had her in my kepyng and at wylle, by a Yere and a Daye after our Marryage, I would not have changed for none other, farer ne fowler, richer ne pourer, ne for none other descended of gretter lynage, sleeping ne waking, at noo time, and if the said B were sole and I sole, I would take her to be my wyfe before all other wymen of the worlde, of what condytion soevere they be, good or evyle, as helpe me God, and Seyntys, and this flesh and all fleshes.

The foregoing words are inscribed below the Flitch. There is a reference to them, in one of Horace Walpole's Letters.

To an applicant who was a "villeyn" corn and a cheese were given in addition to the Flitch. A horse was also provided to take him beyond the limits of the Manor, the free tenants of which were to accompany him with "trompets, tabourets, and other manoir of mynstralcie."

Pennant, who went to "Whichenoure House" in 1780, says the local Flitch had "remained untouched from the first century of its institution to the present." He also avers that "the late and present worthy owners of the Manor were deterred from entering into the holy state from the dread of not obtaining their own Bacon!" The present owner of Wichnor, or Wychnor Park, is Mr. T. B. Levett. The Lord of the Manor is Lord Lichfield. In the Lichfield Road there is a "Flitch of Bacon" inn as there is in Little Dunmow.

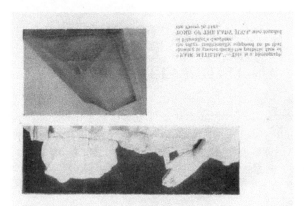

"FAIR MATILDA", TOMB OF THE LADY JUGA

"FAIR MATILDA."—This is a photograph show in greater detail the pathetic face of the effigy traditionally supposed to be that of Fitzwalter's daughter.

TOMB OF THE LADY JUGA, who founded the Priory in 1104.

FISH-POND OF THE MONKS.—Site of one of a remarkable series of fish ponds—it may also be mill-ponds—which extend from near Priory Place.

DETAIL OF CARVING.—From the choir stalls of the church. Note the dying pig, conceivably an allusion by some waggish monk to the Flitch ceremony!

FISH-POND OF THE MONKS, DETAIL OF CARVING

FISH-POND OF THE MONKS.—Site of one of a remarkable series of fish ponds—it may also be mill-ponds—which extend from near Priory Place.

DETAIL OF CARVING.—From the choir stalls of the church. Note the flying pig, conceivably an allusion by some waggish monk to the Flitch ceremony!

CHAPTER XIII

THE BACON OVER SEA

A few years ago Mr. Hastings Worrin, J.P., a churchwarden of the Priory Church of Little Dunmow, and a well-known collector of memorials of the Bacon ceremonies and of the old Priory, to whom the writer of this record is greatly indebted, received a letter addressed to "The Prior of Dunmow." It was from a New York lawyer and his wife, also a member of the legal profession, who had had a little Flitch celebration on their own account, and seemed to think (as the *Times* of August 21, 1803, actually did) that the old Priory still existed—

Whereas, (runs a little fly sheet which they issued to their friends) Girdwood Mulliner and Gabrielle his wife, in reverence for the old tradition, its quaint basic thought so sweetly resting in the sanctity of the marriage relation, knowing in their hearts that they have earned the Flitch of Bacon by the sure right of their living, although far from the Priory and the pointed stones, do here and now kneel and lay claim to it—

I, Leslie Allen Wright, the chief attendant to the Bridegroom upon his day of wedding, praying a grace of pardon for usurping the Prior's rightful duty, yet feeling the fine prompting spirit of the ancient custom, do now bestow upon these two worthy persons, Walter Girdwood Mulliner and Gabrielle his wife, a Flitch of Bacon.

May they in all the added years of their life grow in Ripeness and in Spirit. Amen.

A Bacon custom in Brittany has been referred to. Mention may also be made of a German story, "The Man and the Flitch of Bacon"; also of the Flitch which hung in the old Red Tower of Vienna with doggerel below it which Dr. Bell has thus translated—

Is there to be found a married man
That in verity declare can,
That his marriage him doth not rue,
That he has no fear of his wife for a shrew,
He may this Bacon for himself down hew?

The tale goes that a would-be possessor of the Red Tower Bacon asked, when a ladder had been brought for his assistance, that some one should cut down the Flitch for him, as if he got a grease-spot on his best clothes his wife would scold him! Needless to say, this applicant was not allowed to have the Bacon.

Dr. Bell traces to the earliest times the origin of all customs of hanging up Bacon. Does not Dionysius Halicarnassus mention the presence of a fine Flitch in the chief temple at Alba Longa? Jewellers still sell as charms little pigs of gold, silver and bog oak, and in time past the side of what had once been a sow was no doubt displayed as an emblem of fertility.

APPENDIX

THE LAST PRIOR OF DUNMOW

In the Manuscript Department of the British Museum one may turn over in Latin and in an old English transcript, the household accounts kept by Geoffrey Shether, the last Prior of Dunmow. During the last four years of the Priory's existence, 1531-5, that is up to the time of the dissolution of the minor monasteries, the Prior entered up his accounts every Sunday in a long narrow book such as one sees on bakers' counters.

The entries at the very end of the book are in regard to the payment to one "Purcas"—still a Little Dunmow name—"for iiij days' werke, xxd," and to two "labryng" men for their "werke." Earlier in the book a payment "to my stuarde for kepying of my Curte at Dunmowe" is chronicled. A large proportion of the expenses are in respect of farm work or stock. There is an entry more than once for "stoor bolox." On several occasions expenditure was incurred for the ringing of pigs and the destruction of rats. There are also various sums for work on the steeple.

The fishponds of our illustration do not appear to have yielded all the fish needed by the Priory, for there are two entries for "fyscche" bought. If there is no mention of Bacon, there are "rewardes for venison," and if no allusion occurs to the Flitch ceremony, it was not, apparently, because the Prior would have been above being interested in such a mundane thing, for twice or thrice he puts down "my costs at the feyr," and he gave a "reward to the Lord of Mysrule of Dunmow." Moreover, is there not an entry, "For sugar candy I bowte"?

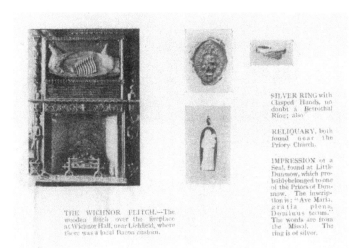

THE WICHNOR FLITCH, SILVER RING, RELIQUARY, IMPRESSION

THE WICHNOR FLITCH.—The wooden flitch over the fireplace at Wichnor Hall, near Lichfield, where there was a local Bacon custom.

SILVER RING with Clasped Hands, no doubt a Betrothal Ring; also

RELIQUARY, both found near the Priory Church.

IMPRESSION of a Seal, found at Little Dunmow, which probably belonged to one of the Priors of Dunmow. The inscription is: "Ave Maria, gratia plena, Dominums tecum." The words are from the Missal. The ring is of silver.

THE PRIORY CHURCH IN ITS SADLY MODERN GUISE.

The Fair Matilda

The story of the poisoning of the Fair Matilda is in the Cotton MS., Cleopatra, C. iii., folio 291 (British Museum), a sixteenth or early seventeenth century copy of or extract from the *Dunmow Chronicle*. The original of the *Chronicle* has not been traced. Tanner in his *Notitia Monastica* does not mention it, but only the Cotton MS. and the Harley MS. referred to in the Introduction to this booklet. The story is entered under the year 1211, in which "mota est discordia inter Regem Johannem et Barones suos occasione Matildis," etc. The Chartulary of Dunmow Priory (page 20), a register of charters, deeds, etc., is quite a different thing from the *Chronicle*, and does not contain the story. The Chartulary is in handwriting of the thirteenth century. The rubric at the beginning gives the date of its compilation as 1275. A few documents have been copied into it at later times.

The photographs of the effigies and of the chair in Little Dunmow Church are by Mr. F. T. Morris, of Felsted; of the modern trial scene and procession by Mr. R. Stacey, of Dunmow; of the Counsel for the Bacon by Mr. J. Willett, of Dunmow; of the rest of the subjects (with the exception of the manuscripts) by Miss Arundel, B.A., of Great Canfield, by kind permission of Mr. Hastings Worrin, J.P., of Little Dunmow, in whose possession they are. The photograph of carving in the Church was taken for Mr. Worrin. The photograph of the fireplace in Wichnor Hall is by Mr. J. S. Simnett, Guild Street, Burton-on-Trent.

For the List of Winners of the Bacon on page 47, we are indebted to the Misses Carter, Dunmow.

Butler & Tanner The Selwood Printing Works Frome and London

9 789362 993670